Living the Ten Commandments

author
Ted Schroeder

table of contents

Session 1: Living Grace-fully in Relationship to God 5

Session 2: Living Grace-fully and Speaking the Truth 23

Session 3: Living Grace-fully and Protecting Others 34

Session 4: Living Grace-fully with Our Parents 47

Session 5: Living Grace-fully in Our Sexuality 58

Session 6: Living Grace-fully with Our Desires 70

Living Gracefully in Relationship to God

Opening Worship

Leader: Blessed is the man who does not walk in the counsel of the wicked or stand in the way of sinners or sit in the seat of mockers.

Group: **But his delight is in the law of the Lord, and on His law he meditates day and night.**

Leader: He is like a tree planted by streams of water, which yields its fruit in season, and whose leaf does not wither. Whatever he does prospers.

Group: **Not so the wicked! They are like chaff that the wind blows away.**

Leader: Therefore the wicked will not stand in the judgment, nor sinners in the assembly of the righteous.

Group: **For the Lord watches over the way of the righteous, but the way of the wicked will perish. (Psalm 1:1-6)**

- **What does it mean to "delight in the law of the Lord"?**

- **In what way are those "happy" or "blessed" who keep God's commandments?**

📖 **Matthew 5:48**

📖 **Matthew 5:17**

📖 **James 1:22-25**

But How Do We Do It?

We live in a world that is running as fast as it can away from God and God's will. People think they find God in themselves and that any means is justified if it serves themselves. In the midst of that kind of a society, how do we live the Christian life according to the will of God?

One way is to limit our understanding of God's will and to do our best to be "righteous." We can work very hard at keeping the law, following the commandments, questioning our every action to see if we have sinned or not. That kind of living might seem "good," but eventually we begin to worry if we're "good" enough. Fear and doubt set in. It becomes a joyless following of the letter of the law—the letter that brings death (2 Corinthians 3:6).

Jesus was once asked what was the "greatest" commandment. He did not choose one of the ten.

📖 **Matthew 22:37-40**

📖 **Romans 13:9-10**

Live in God's Love

To live righteously is to live in God's love. As we live according to the will of God we are constantly renewed by the grace of God. We are aware that we are unable to live perfectly according to the will of God. As we come up against the law of God we constantly find ourselves failing. In that sense the law is our instructor or a mirror that shows us—not just how we have failed—but how desperately we need the Savior.

The secret of righteous living—even in a broken and corrupt world—is to be able to live grace-fully, to look into the "perfect law of God" and to depend on God's grace in Jesus Christ to enable us to live according to that law and will for us.

- **What are some words or phrases that come to mind when you reflect on the word "Law?"**

- **What are some words or phrases that come to mind when you reflect on the word "Gospel?"**

Focusing Our Sight

"But Jeffrey, you can't draw a picture of God. No one knows what God looks like."
"Oh no? Well, they will when I get done."

• **What is there in Jeffrey that is in all of us?**

Looking at the Law

You shall have no other gods.

What does this mean? We should fear, love and trust God above everything else.

You shall not misuse the name of the Lord your God.

What does this mean? We should fear and love God so that we do not curse, swear, use satanic arts, lie, or deceive by His name, but call upon it in every trouble, pray, praise and give thanks.

Remember the Sabbath day by keeping it holy.

What does this mean? We should fear and love God so that we do not despise preaching and His Word, but hold it sacred and gladly hear and learn it.

- **What do these commandments say to you?**

- **What demands do they put on you?**

- Remember Jesus' "first" commandment: "Love the Lord your God with all your heart and soul and mind." Why is keeping that commandment particularly difficult?

Looking at Life

Video 1A

- What were some positive examples of grace-filled living?

- What were some negative examples?

Video 1B

- What were some understandings of a "fulfilled life?"

- How did God and His will play into (or fail to play into) their insights?

- What did law have to do with those definitions?

- What did grace have to do with them?

- What is your definition of "fulfillment" in life?

- What does God's grace have to do with that definition?

Video 1C

- What breaking of the commandments did you see?

- What keeping of the commandments did you see?

- How can you tell that Steve is trying to come to terms with his understanding of God and God's will for him?

- What does he seem to be looking for?

- In your experience, how can God's law seem to become a barrier in our relationships?

- Is anyone willing to share an experience in their life where this became a problem?

- Why is it so difficult to share the good news of God's grace with others, especially members of our own families?

- What advice could you give to Catherine in dealing with Steve?

Video 1D

- How did Steve's doubt affect his outlook on life?

- How did he seem to be missing a sense of being grace-filled?

- How did Patrice's doubt affect her outlook on life? How did she seem to be missing a sense of being grace-filled?

- If you could give advice to Tommy and Miriam in dealing with these struggles, what would you say? How would you evaluate how they did attempt to reach out?

- How does God reach out to those who are struggling with faith?

Living Grace-fully in Relationship to God

The commandment reads, "Love the Lord your God with all your heart and with all your soul and with all your mind" (Matthew 22:37).

- Presently, do you think you love Him more with all your "head" than with your "heart"?

- If your family were to answer the question for you, what would they say?

- What evidence could you give of loving God with your "heart"?

The title of this week's lesson was "Living Grace-fully in Relationship to God." Studies show that Christians often put God in a box after worship and seldom speak to Him or of Him during the rest of the week.

- Is there much "God-talk" in your home, present tense?

- In the last day or two, name some instances of "God-talk" in your home, at your work, with your neighbors, and with your friends.

Video 1E

How would you respond in the spirit of the commandment to each of the following situations?

- Tommy receives a call from work.

- Patrice asks Catherine to "tone down" her message.

- Baines and Steve argue.

Looking to the Word

📖 John 20:24-29

- What sounds "modern" in what Thomas has to say?

- In what sense is Thomas' struggle with doubt our own? *Because we have not seen.*

📖 Acts 9:3-15

- What similarities do you see between the two encounters?

- What differences?

- How is the outcome different or similar?

📖 John 21:15-19

- How is this encounter the same as the other two?

- How is it different?

- What do they all say about our own times of doubt?

- In each case, who approaches whom?

- What does that action say about God's love for us in Christ?

- How can we characterize Jesus' love, even for the wayward?

- Based on the three Bible accounts, how might you express assurance to a "doubter?"

- In what ways do all of us need to hear that assurance?

Fullfillment

📖 **2 Corinthians 4:1, 5-11**

Living in Grace in the Coming Days

Choose one or more activities to complete before the next session.

1. Think of a time in your life when you were struggling with your faith in God or your relationship with Him. Write a letter to yourself at that time. Put in the letter the things you would have wanted to hear and be reassured about during that time. See John 20:24-29, Acts 9:3-15, and John 21:15-19 for insights. Keep the letter in a place where you can find it and read it again when your faith is tested.

2. Set a time to talk with one or two others whose faith life you admire. Find out from them how they are able to live grace-fully. Ask how God is present in their daily living and how God's grace is a part of their relationships.

3. Write the first three commandments on a large piece of paper and post them somewhere in your home. Reflect on how you are living those commandments this week. When have you had to depend on God's grace because of failure? When has God helped you to live grace-fully in keeping the commandments?

4. Watch several "sit-coms" or movies alone or with some others from the class. Try to determine what issues of a relationship to God the stories you see deal with. In what way are these people confronting the commandments? How do they respond to that confrontation?

5. Sunday is just another day for most of the world. What are some ways to make the Sabbath holy? Is there someone from your congregation who didn't make it to Sunday worship and could use some help or cheering up? Could the family do something to enjoy God's creation? Think of a

few more ways to set Sunday apart to try this week or in the weeks to come.

6. Scribes used to illuminate, or highly decorate, passages of scripture while copying them. Have each member of the family pick a favorite verse to illuminate. After sharing the significance of the verse and artwork, post them around the home.

7. God's attributes were revealed with various names throughout the Old Testament. Look up a few and list how you can love and fear God in each of these different character traits, then pray for the Holy Spirit's strength to help you do this.

Why Study the Ten Commandments?

So why bother to study the Ten Commandments? They are, after all, pretty much out of date. These stone-tablet rules from a mountain-top God, aimed at a wandering desert people who lived several thousands of years ago cannot have much to do with us today. Can they?

And besides, are we not people of the Gospel, of the Good News? Do we not affirm that Christ is the end of the Law? Are we not in the business of proclaiming the love and acceptance of God?

That was, after all, what Paul meant when he said that "love is the fulfillment of the law" (Romans 13:10). The Christian was controlled by the living out of a grateful response to God for the gift of forgiveness and salvation in Jesus Christ. That inner control is what James referred to as "the perfect law that gives freedom" (James 1:25). And on the basis of the living out of a grateful response to God, Paul could state that all things were "permissible" to the Christian (1 Corinthians 6:12).

In addition, there was a time when society fostered the "Christian values," based on the Ten Commandments, that encouraged the individual Christian to live out the law of love and the law of God. Personal piety was valued; marriage was the norm; integrity and honesty were a part of what every child learned at home and school; violence was universally abhorred; and the like. But the world has shifted. We live in what many are calling a post-Christian world. Value systems that have nothing to do with the Ten Commandments or the commands of Christ abound.

So again the question: What does the law of God have to do with the life of the Christian in this post-Christian world? How does the Christian find the direction and discipline that he or she needs, not only to be considered a "practicing" Christian, but to carry out the will of God for his or her life?

Unfortunately, too many Christians have given up on the question. If we are in the forgiving business, if God is the kind excuser in the sky, if everyone is basically acceptable to God anyway, then why bother with the commandments at all? Just do your best and it will be all right with God, we seem to say.

And what we end up with is a religiosity that masquerades as faith life. We end up with a community of do-gooders who seem to be in the business of marketing a God who does not really care what we do, what we say, how we behave, as long as we "go to church" and carry through on some of the forms of Christianity.

Dietrich Bonhoeffer calls it "cheap grace." In *The Cost of Discipleship* he says: "Cheap grace is the deadly enemy of the church ... Cheap grace means grace as a doctrine, a principle, a system ... Cheap grace means justification of sin without the justification of the sinner. Cheap grace is the preaching of forgiveness without requiring repentance, baptism without church discipline, Communion without confession, absolution without contrition. Cheap grace is ... grace without Jesus Christ, living and incarnate."

But the solution to the cheap grace problem is not to return to a more strident preaching of the law. Scolding, making Christians feel guilty, bashing them with the commandments at every turn will not make them more sincere, more dedicated or even better behaved.

Both ways to discipleship are doomed to failure: cheap grace leads to religion without faith and faith without Christ. Yet, "laying down the law" leads to better behaved Christians who are dragged down and defeated by an unmerciful God who constantly harangues them with demands they cannot fulfill and conditional promises they cannot receive.

The solution to the dilemma is to do what Christians have always done: To look into the perfect mirror of the law, to see ourselves and our needs and our failings and faults clearly when held up against the perfect demands of God's law. The Ten Commandments were interpreted by Jesus in the sermon on the Mount: "Be perfect" (Matthew 5:48). And then after looking in that mirror, to run to the perfect Gospel of Jesus Christ where we are forgiven and set free to live the life to which God is calling us.

And so we look at the ancient law of God. Not as a curiosity. Certainly not as a way of "getting right with God." Not as a way to impress others or to begin a better social order. We constantly come to the law with the question: As a child of God, what is God's will for me in this situation? And when we have discerned that will, seeking the Spirit's help to live according to God's will. Because it does matter what we do. It does matter when we ignore God's will and live our own way. It does matter when we set off on our own course and no longer hear God's call to perfect living. It does matter—and it is called sin.

And it does matter what we do when confronted with that sin. The route to a new life, a new chance, to resurrection is not trying harder to keep the law nor pressing ourselves more earnestly to get in line with the will of God. It is the gracious, Good

News that in Christ we are forgiven and free to live according to the perfect will of God.

In this course, we will listen to God's law again—but not in the abstract. We will not be asked to affirm the commandments or to think through how they might apply to this lawless world we live in. In this course we will practice the grace-full art of confronting God's will as it touches our daily lives. We will think through what the discipline of the law of God means as we make choices, deal with people, face options, make our way in the world. And we'll do this as we look into the lives of others who, like us, are living under and attempting to live out "the perfect law of liberty," the will of God for them.

Preparing for Session 2: Living Grace-fully and Speaking the Truth

An old saying goes: "Intelligent people talk about ideas, average people talk about happenings, and stupid people talk about people." If that is true, many of us probably fall in the "stupid" group. It is easy to talk about others. Other people do such foolish things. And when we do talk about them, we make ourselves look so much better. "Compared to that person," we seem to say, "I'm practically a saint." But being practically a saint in comparison to someone else is not the way of grace-filled living.

Jesus said that the second great commandment is "Love your neighbor as yourself." The remaining commandments show us what it means to love neighbor as self. Based on our relationship to God, we deal with our neighbor in love. Jesus indicates that "love for one another" is the true evidence of discipleship (John 13:35). Because He loved us, we love, and we keep our promises, honor parents, protect other's property, and the like.

The commandment to not give false testimony is one of the more difficult commandments, although none are easy to keep.

Our competitive world pressures us to take any advantage we can over others. If we don't, we are told, they will take advantage of us. Our world considers it foolish to give things away, to fail to protect what is ours, to put other's needs first. If we would truly live the love to which Christ calls us, we would be considered fools or worse by the rest of the world.

Jesus knows the struggle. "Don't be surprised," he says, "if the world hates you" (John 15:18). Part of the reason for that hatred is that as Christ's people we refuse to go along with what others tell us is "normal." When we refuse to use either the truth or lies to get an advantage over someone else, we may be ridiculed or even excluded by those who consider attacking someone else as a standard operating procedure.

Not doing something is tough enough, but it is difficult to go beyond that into positive action as well. It is difficult to look at the failings and faults of those who seem to be in competition with us and to "put the best construction" on their acts. It is difficult to defend our neighbor when he doesn't seem to deserve it. It seems unfair to have to protect another's good name, when that person does not even seem to care about it. So difficult, in fact, that once again, we are not going to be able to keep the commandment on our own. We don't have the wisdom, or the insight, or the love for our neighbor to do it on our own.

The only way we are going to be able to keep this commandment is by the grace of God. When we live grace-fully, we know that we are loved, defended and rescued by Jesus Himself. We know that we are forgiven and free to live in the love that we have been shown. Even as we deal with the words that come out of our mouth, we are challenged to live grace-fully.

Living Gracefully and Speaking the Truth

Opening Worship

Leader: Blessed are they whose ways are blameless, who walk according to the law of the Lord.

Group: Blessed are they who keep His statutes and seek Him with all their heart. They do nothing wrong; they walk in His ways.

Leader: You have laid down precepts that are to be fully obeyed.

Group: Oh, that my ways were steadfast in obeying Your decrees!

Leader: Then I would not be put to shame when I consider all Your commands.

Group: I will praise You with an upright heart as I learn Your righteous laws.

Leader: I will obey Your decrees; do not utterly forsake me.

Group: How can a young man keep his way pure? By living according to Your word.

Leader: I seek you with all my heart; do not let me stray from Your commands.

Group: **I have hidden Your word in my heart that I might not sin against You.**

Leader: Praise be to You, O Lord; teach me Your decrees.

Group: **With my lips I recount all the laws that come from Your mouth.**

Leader: I rejoice in following Your statutes as one rejoices in great riches.

Group: **I meditate on Your precepts and consider Your ways.**

Leader: I delight in Your decrees; I will not neglect Your word.

Group: **Do good to Your servant, and I will live; I will obey Your word.**

Leader: Open my eyes that I may see wonderful things in Your law (Psalm 119:1-18).

Review

Video 2A

• **What insights did you gain from and since the last session?**

Focusing Our Sight

📖 **Proverbs 22:1**

• **What are some ways this proverb is true?**

"Tell the media he cheats on his wife and beats his children."
"We've no proof. How do we know it's the truth?"

"Proof? Truth? What do they have to do with anything?"

- **Even though we know it is harmful, why is it so often easy for us to share or listen to gossip?**

- **To what extent is it possible to destroy someone's good name with a "good story" these days? To what extent does the accusation become the conviction?**

- **Is this type of behavior encouraged by society?**

- **Does a "good story" operate the same way in an office? In a home? In a congregation?**

Looking at the Law

You shall not give false testimony against your neighbor.

What does this mean? We should fear and love God so that we do not tell lies about our neighbor, betray him, slander him, or hurt his reputation, but defend him, speak well of him, and explain everything in the kindest way.

Matthew 7:1-5

Looking at Life

Video 2B

- Why do you think Jerry became angry and verbally abusive of Julia?

- Was anything Jerry said the truth?

- What might be some of the reasons Baines says Jerry's like "King Kong on speed, but he's not that smart?"

- Did Baines say anything that was true?

- What reasons could Julia have for saying, "Not all of us are perfect," and calling Patrice an "ice queen"?

- Was Julia speaking the truth?

📖 Ephesians 4:14-16
📖 Ephesians 4:29
- What does it mean to speak the truth in love?

- What are some of the differences Tommy and Miriam perceive in Carrie's needs?

- Whose attitude do you think is the most helpful for Carrie?

- How do we know when we are being helpful or harmful?

- What are some situations that people or you yourself have faced where even though the truth may hurt, it still needs to be spoken?

📖 Galatians 5:22-26

- What are the tools that the Holy Spirit gives us to help us live grace-fully in our relationships?

- How does our attitude toward ourselves and our grace-filled relationship to God shape how we form attitudes about others?

Video 2C

- Miriam has agreed to be a job reference for Carrie. In this situation, what "witness" could be helpful and what "witness" could be harmful?

- Catherine is willing to boost the numbers in order to help her cause. When we "shade" the truth, where are we putting our trust?

- **Julia again defames Patrice. If you could write one sentence of grace-filled Christian advice for Julia to post in front of her on her desk, what would it be?**

- **What are some things we can do when someone is being defamed in our presence?**

Role play how you would offer grace-filled advice and speak to the person in love regarding his/her situation.

- Miriam agrees to be a reference for Carrie. - *He who rebukes a man will in the end gain more favor than he who has a flattering tongue (Proverbs 28:23).*

- Catherine is trying to take things into her own hands and "shade" the truth in order to make the center look better. - *Do not say "I'll pay you for this wrong!" Wait for the Lord, and he will deliver you (Proverbs 20:22).*

- Julia cuts down Patrice and shares knowledge of her past to Steve and Miriam. - *He who covers an offense promotes love, but he who repeats the matter separates close friends (Proverbs 17:9).*

- Steve defends Patrice. - *Pleasant words are a honeycomb, sweet to the soul and healing to the bones (Proverbs 16:24).*

Video 2D

- What might be the long-term result of Julia setting aside her hurt?

- Why is this difficult?

- What benefit does God intend for you by giving you this commandment?

Acting Grace-fully

I do not understand what I do. For what I want to do I do not do, but what I hate I do ... For I have the desire to do what is good, but I cannot carry it out ... What a wretched man I am! Who will rescue me? ... Thanks be to God—through Jesus Christ our Lord! ... Therefore, there is now no condemnation for those who are in Christ Jesus (Romans 7:15, 18b, 24-25, 8:1).

Living Grace-fully and Speaking Truth

Statistics tell us that 91% of Americans lie regularly.

- In the last few days, can you think of some lies you've heard? How about from your own mouth?

- Even though you may not be able to think of any lies you've spoken recently, why are you glad for "grace"?

In the hymn, "Take My Life, O Lord, Renew," we sing, "Take my lips and keep them true, Filled with messages from You."

- Name some times today, tomorrow, and this week when it would be valuable for you to pray these words (e.g., before you spoke with your mother-in-law or with your son's teacher).

- Share why you might have difficulty with you words at these times.

Video 2E

How would you respond in the spirit of the commandment to each of the following situations?

- Miriam receives a phone call.

- Catherine is met by reporters.

Living in Grace in the Coming Days

Choose one or more activities to complete before the next session.

1. This week listen when people are talking about someone else. See if you can say something positive when you hear something negative. Think of one person in your home, office, church or community who needs to be championed. Pray for guidance and focus on how to be positive when that person comes up in conversation. Notice the reactions of the people around you and how it affects what they say.

2. Very often what we say is correct or true but the way we say it is not. This week examine your tone of voice and attitude when speaking. Is there someone you are unusually harsh with? Are you speaking the truth? Is it with a helpful, loving attitude and tone of voice?

3. Read through the newspaper or news magazine. Look for examples of telling the truth and speaking falsely and what the long term effects are. How could things continue to ripple out?

4. Look up "truth" in a Bible dictionary or concordance. Pick a handful of the references and read them. What can you summarize from the list of texts and the scripture you read?

Preparing for Session 3: Living Grace-fully and Protecting Others

At first, the commandment to not murder seems easy to keep. Even in our violent world, statistically there are few murders. Even though murders in a large city like Chicago number in the hundreds, millions of people live in the same city day after day and do not murder one another. And though we may get angry with others occasionally, and though that anger can reach a fever pitch in some cases, few of us would even contemplate actually causing another's death.

But before we get too comfortable, just as the people in Jesus' day seemed to be comfortable with their ability to "keep the law," Jesus has another word for us about this commandment: **"You have heard that it was said to the people long ago, 'Do not murder, and anyone who murders will be subject to judgment.' But I tell you that anyone who is angry with his brother will be subject to judgment. Again, anyone who says to his brother, 'Raca,' is answerable to the Sanhedrin. But anyone who says, 'You fool!' will be in danger of the fire of hell"** (Matthew 5:21-22).

Suddenly Jesus has made keeping the law not only difficult but virtually impossible. Who has not gotten angry or said an angry word to another? Who has not insulted another? If we are "liable to the judgment" for our angry words or for our sharp tongue then who can keep the commandment?

The commandment that started out so easy to keep becomes an immense task. How can we defend others in a world that is out to harm us? How can we help and sustain others when often they don't deserve it? How can we avoid anger when others speak angrily to us? How can we avoid insult when we are insulted? Is God serious about this commandment?

God is serious indeed. Our failure to live up to the high standards God has set does not set aside the commandment. Again, we realize that if we are to keep the commandment, it will only be by the grace of God. When we live grace-fully, when we live the life of the forgiven and free child of God, we can cherish and protect not only ourselves, but the life and health of others as well.

Living Gracefully and Protecting Others

Opening Worship

Leader: Praise the Lord, O my soul; all my inmost being, praise His holy name.

Group: Praise the Lord, O my soul, and forget not all His benefits—

Leader: who forgives all your sins and heals all your diseases,

Group: who redeems your life from the pit and crowns you with love and compassion,

Leader: who satisfies your desires with good things so that your youth is renewed like the eagle's.

Group: The Lord works righteousness and justice for all the oppressed.

Leader: He made known His ways to Moses, His deeds to the people of Israel:

Group: The Lord is compassionate and gracious, slow to anger, abounding in love.

Leader: He will not always accuse, nor will He harbor His anger forever;

Group: He does not treat us as our sins deserve or repay us according to our iniquities.

Leader: For as high as the heavens are above the earth, so great is His love for those who fear Him;

Group: as far as the east is from the west, so far has He removed our transgressions from us.

Leader: As a father has compassion on his children, so the Lord has compassion on those who fear Him (Psalm 103: 1-13).

Review

Video 3A

• **What insights did you gain from and since the last session?**

Focusing Our Sight

📖 **Luke 10:30-36**

• **How different would the world be if everyone had the attitude of the Good Samaritan?**

• **How would it impact our individual daily lives?**

Looking at the Law

You shall not murder.

What does this mean? We should fear and love God so that we do not hurt or harm our neighbor in his body, but help and support him in every physical need.

📖 Matthew 5:21-22

Looking at Life

Video 3B

• Do you think a majority or a minority of people in society would feel the same way Julia does about Jerry?

• What criteria do you think Julia used to determine Jerry's value?

• Define prejudice.

- What groups of people in our society are considered of little value?

- What criteria are used to judge them? Does Julia use similar criteria?

- Are similar criteria used to judge people in our families? our church?

- When judged to be of little value, how are these people treated?

📖 Ephesians 2:4-7
- What Does God say about the value of Jerry and every human being?

- Why is it so difficult for us to reflect this attitude?

- What gives us the power to reflect this attitude?

📖 **Ephesians 4:26**

Video 3C

- Did Catherine have a legitimate reason to be angry with the mechanic?

- When did Catherine's anger become sin?

- Did Julia have a legitimate reason to be angry with Wayne?

- When did Julia's anger become sin?

- Does Baines have a legitimate reason to be angry with his father?

- When did his anger turn to sin?

- How might past experience have affected Julia's reaction?

- How might past experiences have affected Baines' reaction?

- What are other situations in our lives where past experiences can affect current behavior?

- What caution should we have when we feel like we've "been there done that?"

A stone thrown into water will create a circular ripple of waves. Discuss the potential "ripple effect" of the following actions:

- **Catherine's treatment of the mechanic.**

- **Julia's treatment of Wayne.**

- **Baines treatment of his father.**

📖 **Ephesians 4:31-32, 5:1-2**

- **What motivates Christians to be kind and compassionate?**

- **What does it mean to be kind and compassionate, even when we have a legitimate reason to be angry?**

*"Sir, I'll be getting off at the next stop,
if you would like to have this seat."*

Video 3D

- **What did Baines' dream help him realize?**

- **What would it mean for Baines to treat his father with kindness and compassion?**

- **What is Julia starting to realize about Wayne?**

- **What might she also realize about herself?**

- **How should Baines' father's or the mechanic's reactions affect how they should be treated?**

Video 3E

Julia and Catherine were able to forgive shortcomings in Wayne and the mechanic. Each is trying to "hate the action without hating the person."

- **How will this change Julia's behavior?**

- What "ripple effect" might it cause?

- How will Catherine's treatment of the mechanic change?

- What will the "ripple effect" likely be if Baines changes his behavior toward his father?

For you were once darkness, but now you are light in the Lord. Live as children of light (for the fruit of the light consists in all goodness, righteousness and truth) and find out what pleases the Lord (Ephesians 5:8-10).

Living Grace-fully and Protecting Others

In the commandment we studied today, we learned that we can "murder" people with our words.

- Think of the people you have contact with today and throughout this week. Are you speaking words to them or others that might be "murdering" them?

- **Think of some people you have teased in your lifetime who perhaps have been terribly damaged because of your words and the words of others. How easy would it be for you to sit down today and write a letter of apology or pick up the telephone and ask for his/her forgiveness? How does "grace" fit into all of this?**

Often you will hear people lament, "People have lost all respect for life." The word "respect" can mean to see another through the eyes of God.

- **Keeping in mind this definition, what are some specific things you can do today to show greater "respect" for life?**

Video 3F

How would you respond in the spirit of the commandment to each of the following situations?

- **Tommy overhears Baines' comments.**

- **Julia is given a pile of files.**

- **Catherine recognizes a person who harmed her.**

Living in Grace in the Coming Days

The following activities are designed to help you identify areas in your life where God desires you to reflect His love. Choose one or more to complete during the week.

1. Seek out an opportunity to be a Good Samaritan. Is there someone in a nearby hospital or nursing home who would like a cheerful, caring person to visit? Does a family need meals or transportation due to a parent who is ill or injured? Is there a shut-in connected with your congregation in need of a visit? Notice your reaction, the reaction of the one you helped, and the reactions of others in the area.

2. Look at the news media and find examples of those living out the call to care for and protect others. How are they treated by the news? By society in general? Are there plenty of examples or just a few? How can you follow their example?

3. Take note this week of prejudice that surrounds us. Make a list of all of the statements, actions, pictures, and news reports that have some kind of prejudice connected with them. How many are right in our homes? How many are global? How is the "ripple effect" helping to perpetuate them? What can we do to combat them?

Preparing for Session 4: Living Grace-fully with Our Parents

"Love your neighbor as yourself" was the second greatest commandment given by Jesus. And the place to start looking for the neighbor we are to love is in our home. Our first and fundamental relationships are with parents and family. Our sense of ourselves and our religious faith are cradled there. Our ability to survive both physically and spiritually depends on our relationship to our parents.

St. Paul takes up the commandment to honor our parents in his explanation of what it means to live as "children of the light."

Chapter 5 of Ephesians starts with this challenge: **"Be imitators of God, therefore, as dearly loved children and live a life of love, just as Christ loved us and gave himself up for us as a fragrant offering and sacrifice to God."** (verses 1-2). Paul goes on to describe what the relationships will be among those who live a life of love. He says, **"Children, obey your parents in the Lord, for this is right. 'Honor your father and mother'—which is the first commandment with a promise—'that it may go well with you and that you may enjoy long life on the earth.'"** (6:1-3).

Keeping this commandment goes far beyond simply giving honor to parents when they are elderly. Keeping this commandment means that we are to make God's giving love the very heart of our relationships in our homes. We are not only to honor our parents and others in authority, but to obey them—respect them as representatives of God with us.

At first, keeping the commandment to honor our parents seems easy. After all, everyone loves his/her parents. Parents naturally seek the best for their children. Christian homes are characterized by their loving relationships—at least we hope they are. But the family is under terrible attack in our world. Violence is a part of too many homes—even Christian homes. Children are often discounted, damaged, misused, abused. Marriages seem to be held together by nothing more than good intentions. Children have lost respect for their elders. The problem is so bad that even political parties try to make points by talking about "restoring the family."

And for all the alarmists and the political blather, we know that families are not going to get better because we make better laws or organize better social programs. What will renew families is the same thing that renews us daily in our relationship with God. It is God's giving love and forgiveness that renews families. Family ministry—ministry in and with families is the living out of the forgiving and renewing love of God in our homes. And that can only be done by the grace of God that for-gives and renews us each day.

If living grace-fully is our goal, then the place to start that liv-ing is at home in our relationships to parents, with children and to other members of our family and in relationship to others given primary authority over us.

Living Gracefully with Our Parents

Opening Worship

Leader: I lift up my eyes to the hills— where does my help come from?

Group: My help comes from the Lord, the Maker of heaven and earth.

Leader: He will not let your foot slip— He who watches over you will not slumber;

Group: indeed, He who watches over Israel will neither slumber nor sleep.

Leader: The Lord watches over you— the Lord is your shade at your right hand;

Group: the sun will not harm you by day, nor the moon by night.

Leader: The Lord will keep you from all harm— He will watch over your life;

Group: the Lord will watch over your coming and going both now and forevermore (Psalm 121).

Review

Video 4A

- **What insights did you gain from and since the last session?**

Focusing Our Sight

Calvin and Hobbes

by Bill Watterson

- **What point does this cartoon make about family life?**

Looking at the Law

> ## Honor your father and your mother.
>
> What does this mean? We should fear and
> love God so that we do not despise or anger
> our parents and other authorities, but honor
> them, serve and obey them, love and cherish
> them.

📖 **Ephesians 6:1-3**

Looking at Life

Video 4B

- **What does Tommy's struggle with his firm have to do with this commandment?**

- **How is "that it may go well with you" expressed through Kendall's simple act of washing the car?**

- **How do you think Baines should respond to his father concerning the check?**

📖 Romans 13:1-3, 5

- Who establishes authorities?

- How do we benefit from obeying authorities?

- In verse 5, what does "because of conscience" mean?

📖 Acts 4:18-20

- What boundary does this passage set for Christian obedience?

Video 4C

- Miriam says that she's a "pragmatist." "Some authorities are worthy of being listened to, and some aren't." Why do you agree or disagree?

- Does Steve's mother have a "right" to question his plans?

- According to this commandment, what is Baines' responsibility to his father?

- What responsibility do adult children have to obey their parents?

What would an "honorable" response be in each of the following situations?

- Kara is 20 and living at home between college semesters. Her parents have given her an 11:30 p.m. curfew which she finds unreasonable.
- Cindy and Jeff have 2 children and live in the same city as Jeff's parents. When not with Cindy's parents on alternating years, they celebrate Christmas mornings at Jeff's parents' home. Tradition is very important to Jeff's mother. Cindy and Jeff have decided they want to start their own family tradition and celebrate Christmas morning in their own home.
- Cameron's father is rarely complimentary of him. He wasn't when Cameron was a child and still isn't although Cameron is now in his 40's. Achievements have never seemed good enough. Every time he is with his father, he makes no bones about telling Cameron "If only you had ..." Cameron is considering not going to an upcoming family reunion in order to avoid his father.

Respect

Video 4D
- **Why do you think Steve agreed to stay with a friend instead of with Miriam?**

- Julia tells Baines, " You don't have to be a slave to the past." In what way has Baines become a slave to the past?

📖 Romans 5:6-11
- How can seeing parents as sinners like ourselves help us reconcile a damaged relationship?

- What freedom could forgiveness bring to Baines and his father?

- Even if his father doesn't change, how is it possible for Baines to still experience freedom?

Living Grace-fully with Our Parents

There are few things more painful than for someone to regret not having spoken words of love to someone before he/she died.

- If your parents are still alive, how long has it been since you have told them "I love you"?

- **What do you think this commandment says to children about caring for their aged parents?**

- **What do you expect of your children some day? Have you spoken to them about such a time?**

Video 4E

How would you respond in the spirit of the commandment to each of the following situations?

- **Baines receives a call from his father.**

    How would you react to Baines' father if ...

    - he wanted you to have lunch with him and his new girlfriend?

    - he was revising his will?

    - he was going in for medical tests?

- **Tommy's boss makes demands.**

- Earlier in the video, we learned that Tommy's job kept him from church and family activities. At what point do respecting and obeying those in authority over us conflict with God's desires?

  ○ Isaac's point of view

Living in Grace in the Coming Days

Do one or more of the activities listed below.

1. Write a letter to one or both of your parents thanking them for the role they have played in your life.

2. Read 1 Corinthians 13:1-13. Read verses 4-7 again. What one thing listed do you feel you have the most difficulty expressing to your parents? Write a letter to God. Detail your own behavior and how it makes you feel. Then ask for the Holy Spirit to empower you to behave differently the next time you are faced with the situation.

3. List some people you know who seem to have healthy family relationships. Interview two of them and ask them what their "secrets" are. How are they able to keep their relationships alive and growing? What does their faith in Christ have to do with that growing?

4. Choose one of the following stories of Biblical family relationships and read it carefully. What can we learn about effective family living from these examples? How did their dependence on God (or lack of it) affect their relationships?

   • Abraham and Isaac (Genesis 22:1-14)
   • Joseph and his brothers (Genesis 37, 39–45)
   • Jacob and Esau (Genesis 25:19-34, 27)
   • Ruth and Naomi (Ruth 1–4)

5. Read the texts below together. Make speaking words of repentance to each other for past hurts and forgiveness for Jesus' sake part of your devotional time this week.

   • Matthew 6:14-15
   • Colossians 3:12-13
   • 1 John 1:9

Preparing for Session 5: Living Grace-fully in Our Sexuality

Like some of the others, the commandment to not commit adultery is under siege in our "grab the gusto," individualistic society. Messages that encourage quests for instant gratification undermine any attempt to preserve the intention of this commandment. Sex has become a merchandising tool, an excuse for adolescent humor on TV, and an expected feature of almost any boy/girl encounter. Sexually explicit material is available on our televisions, in the local convenience store and on the Internet. The message of the "joys" of casual sex bombard us and our children. Sexual relationships that in past generations would not have been mentioned now confront us at every turn. People openly boast of their sexual exploits, and growing percentages of adolescents are becoming "sexually active."

The results of the devaluation of sex is not only empty sexual activity, but the attitude also contributes directly to the destabilization of marriage and the disintegration of the home. This commandment assumes a permanent marriage commitment. The commandment condemns, not just wayward sexual activity, but specifically the breaking of the marriage promise. And in a society where the marriage commitment has become a kind of tentative arrangement, the stability of the family disappears.

The latest research indicates that children develop best, emotionally and physically, when they grow up in a secure home where both parents love and nurture them. The homes where that can happen are becoming more rare. More than half of children born to young mothers are born outside the marriage relationship. Millions of children are being raised in single parent homes or reconstituted homes where the "other parent" is not the natural father or mother.

Given the sexual disintegration all around us, this commandment almost sounds anachronistic. Maybe it was meant to apply to a different time— a time when intact families were more vital to individual survival, a time when women and children were more like property. Maybe we do live in a different age— an age of experimentation and immediate reward. Maybe the commandment doesn't fit any more.

And yet we also know from psychological studies that human beings find fulfillment only in relationships that are built on an unconditional love. Conditional love— a love that says I will stay with you or cherish you only as long as you give me what I want or need— is simply destructive. Children who grow up under a conditional parental love grow up feeling unloved. Marriages based on a conditional love come apart at the first time of testing. And our world is filled with lonely people, products of broken homes and broken relationships, wandering about looking for the person who will give them all they think they need. And because they cannot give themselves, they will never find that person.

Unconditional, uncompromising, eternal, powerful, secure, committed love is what this commandment calls for. A posture of giving, of respect, of putting the other person first is the only way it can be kept. Of ourselves, given the world we live in, we don't have a chance of creating that kind of love. That love is God's love, and in relationship to Him we receive and are empowered to give a love to one another that does not give up.

"Love never fails," St. Paul tells us. The love that God creates and shares with us never ends. **"And now these three remain: faith, hope and love,"** he says, **"but the greatest of these is love"** (1 Corinthians 13:8, 13).

Living Gracefully in Our Sexuality

Opening Worship

Leader: Have mercy on me, O God, according to Your unfailing love;

Group: according to Your great compassion blot out my transgressions.

Leader: Wash away all my iniquity and cleanse me from my sin.

Group: For I know my transgressions, and my sin is always before me.

Leader: Against You, You only, have I sinned and done what is evil in Your sight, so that You are proved right when You speak and justified when You judge.

Group: Surely I was sinful at birth, sinful from the time my mother conceived me.

Leader: Surely You desire truth in the inner parts; You teach me wisdom in the inmost place.

Group: Cleanse me with hyssop, and I will be clean; wash me, and I will be whiter than snow.

Leader: Let me hear joy and gladness; let the bones You have crushed rejoice.

Group: **Hide Your face from my sins and blot out all my iniquity.**

Leader: Create in me a pure heart, O God, and renew a steadfast spirit within me.

Group: **Do not cast me from Your presence or take Your Holy Spirit from me.**

Leader: Restore to me the joy of Your salvation and grant me a willing spirit, to sustain me.

Group: **Then I will teach transgressors Your ways, and sinners will turn back to You** (Psalm 51:1-13).

Review

Video 5A

• **What insights did you gain from and since the last session?**

Focusing Our Sight

"We are planning the best wedding for our daughter. Paris designer gowns, orchids from Hawaii, seven course catered dinner. After all, a girl only get married three or four times in her life."

- **In your experience how prevelant in this attitude about marriage?**

Looking at the Law

You shall not commit adultery.

What does this mean? We are to fear and love God so that we lead a sexually pure life in what we say and do, and husband and wife love and honor each other.

📖 **Matthew 5:27-28**
- **How would you rephrase Jesus' words for a teenager?**

Looking at Life

Video 5B

- **Was teasing Patrice about her get-away weekend appropriate or inappropriate? Why or why not?**

- **What different attitudes were expressed concerning sexual activity?**

- **Which ones do you think are realistic?**

Video 5C

- How do you think Tommy would have reacted if his 14-year-old son Kendall had teased Miriam in the same manner he did?

- In the spirit of the commandment, what are realistic boundaries for making sexually-related comments?

📖 Ecclesiastes 4:12

📖 Philippians 4:13

- How does a relationship with Christ help us live out our marriage commitments?

Video 5D

- In Steve's estimation, Miriam demonstrates an "old fashioned" attitude toward sex outside of marriage. What kind of pressures might a person like Miriam deal with?

- What does it take to build up the kind of commitment Miriam has?

- What are things we can do to help children develop a conviction, like Miriam, to stand up to the pressures of the world and live a God pleasing life?

- How might Julia's actions be a form of adultery?

- What advice would you give her?

To remain healthy, relationships need to be nurtured. Job and family are both important commitments. On their own, participating in each individual may seem like the "right" choice. However, when you add them all up, they can create a schedule that leaves little time for the marriage relationship. A common wedding symbol is three rings, signifying husband, wife, and Christ. Nurturing the three of these at once will strengthen the marriage relationship and in turn the family. The Lord Himself tells us that a cord of three strands is not easily broken (Ecclesiastes 4:12).

Video 5E

- What are some possible long-term results for Tommy after realizing that Miriam felt harassed?

- What possible long-term results are there for Miriam in living out God's will for her sexuality?

📖 1 Corinthians 13:4-7

Living Grace-fully in Our Sexuality

A major concern of many families is the proliferation of sexually oriented materials on television programs, in advertising, through Internet.

- **Sex is a wonderful gift from God; however, what's wrong with the way sexuality is being presented in many of the above mentioned formats?**

- **What opportunities do your children or children's children have in your home to get the wrong view of sex? the correct view (God's perspective)?**

- **What changes could you make today that would help you and your children get a clearer view of God's perspective on sexuality?**

- **Lest we think only our children, our grandchildren, or others might be skewed in their thinking because of the things they listen to or watch, in what ways might you yourself be endangering your spiritual well-being by what you're reading or watching?**

When you go home today, review the different things in your home, from the television you watch to the literature you read, and ask, "Do any of these things keep me from leading a pure life?" Then pray for God's grace and help in better being able to keep this commandment.

Video 5F

- **The women discuss men.**

  How is this conversation sexual harassment?

  How would you respond to this conversation?

- **Julia receives a phone call.**

  What would you do if you were Julia?

  What would you do if you were Al?

Living in Grace in the Coming Days

Do one or more of the activities suggested before your next session.

1. Think about each of your children's mate. Considering that they will be relatively the same age, make a list of what you would like your child's future spouse to be learning, and how you would like them to behave. Then consider your children's future in-laws. What are they hoping your children are learning and doing now? Commit to pray for each of your children and their future spouses this week.

2. Write a list of elements of a relationship that are necessary for a successful marriage. The list might include respect, love, hope, self-sacrifice, etc. Then rank them from the most important to the least. Share it with your spouse. Think up a way to share your lists with your children, their friends, and others (maybe young people you know who are planning to get married).

3. Look at 1 Corinthians 13 with your spouse. With this as a guide, write a new set of vows, beginning each with "I promise ..." Talk about ways the promises might be used in a marriage renewal ceremony or to explain the marriage promises to your children.

4. Plan a marriage anniversary celebration that would be particularly meaningful for you or for those you love. What elements capture the commitment and meaning in a marriage? What evidence is there of the reality of struggling and the sufficiency of God?

5. Make a list of everything scheduled for the next week, including work, activities with the kids and other commitments. Look at them in terms of relationships. Are any of them designed to strengthen your marriage (or boyfriend/ girlfriend relationship)? Think up two events that would help build both of you up and schedule them.

Preparing for Session 6: Living Grace-fully with Our Desires

"You shall not steal." In our world, we ought to make it into a banner and hang it everywhere. "Stop stealing, you thieves, you crooks, you cheaters, you manipulators! Stop stealing from the weak and the elderly! Stop taking what is not yours! Stop ripping off the world for your own benefit!" If there ever was a commandment for our grasping, greedy, "get mine first" world— this is it. We need this commandment— there are so many dishonest people out there. We need this commandment to protect our own collection of "mine."

But just about the time we feel a little comfortable that the commandment doesn't really apply to us, Jesus throws a bomb into our comfortable pile of "my stuff." To the rich young man, who by his own admission had "kept the commandments from his youth" Jesus says, **"One thing you lack. Go, sell every-thing you have and give to the poor, and you will have trea-sure in heaven. Then come, follow me"** (Mark 10:21).

Can He really mean that? Is that just some shock tactic for a complacent rich man, or does Jesus saying have something to do with us? **"Then Jesus said to His disciples, 'If anyone would come after Me, he must deny himself and take up his cross and follow Me. For whoever wants to save his life will lose it, but whoever loses his life for Me will find it. What good will it be for a man if he gains the whole world, yet forfeits his soul? Or what can a man give in exchange for his soul?'"** (Matthew 16:24-26).

We are commanded to protect our neighbor's property. Indeed we are commanded to not even to yearn for what another per-son has. But simply avoiding taking or seeking to take what someone else has doesn't set us right with the things that sur-round us. Jesus warns the rich young man and warns us that the real trouble with the stuff we might obtain is that it will in the end really own us. We are always in danger of becoming a slave to our stuff.

When the things we own own us, we lose focus on the grace-full life to which we are called. We have to tend our stuff and increase it. We have to pay attention to getting and enhancing and protecting—and there is little time left for crosses or following or giving or sharing. The commandment protects other's things. But Jesus wants the commandment also to warn us that the world full of good things around us, the beckoning of all the glittery things in the world there are to want and to own, can destroy us spiritually.

Grace-full living, in the light of these commandments, helps our neighbors protect what they have and helps us live life free from the bondage of things.

Living Gracefully with Our Desires

Opening Worship

Leader: Now when He saw the crowds, He went up on a mountainside and sat down. His disciples came to Him,

Group: and He began to teach them, saying:

Leader: "Blessed are the poor in spirit,

Group: for theirs is the kingdom of heaven.

Leader: Blessed are those who mourn,

Group: for they will be comforted.

Leader: Blessed are the meek,

Group: for they will inherit the earth.

Leader: Blessed are those who hunger and thirst for righteousness,

Group: for they will be filled.

Leader: Blessed are the merciful,

Group: for they will be shown mercy.

Leader: Blessed are the pure in heart,

Group: **for they will see God.**

Leader: Blessed are the peacemakers,

Group: **for they will be called sons of God.**

Leader: Blessed are those who are persecuted because of right-eousness,

Group: **for theirs is the kingdom of heaven.**

Leader: Blessed are you when people insult you, persecute you and falsely say all kinds of evil against you because of me.

Group: **Rejoice and be glad, because great is your reward in heaven, for in the same way they persecuted the prophets who were before you.**

Leader: You are the salt of the earth. But if the salt loses its saltiness, how can it be made salty again? It is no longer good for anything, except to be thrown out and trampled by men.

Group: **You are the light of the world. A city on a hill can-not be hidden. Neither do people light a lamp and put it under a bowl. Instead they put it on its stand, and it gives light to everyone in the house.**

Leader: In the same way, let your light shine before men, that they may see your good deeds and praise your Father in heaven" (Matthew 5:1-16).

- **In what ways are Jesus' words here a summary of what we have been studying?**

- How can we be salt and light in the world?

- How do we give glory to God in all that we say and do?

Review

Video 6A

- What insights did you gain from and since the last session?

Make a list of things you hope to achieve in the next 10 years, and what it will take to get there.

- What attitude towards things does the bumper sticker represent?

- What are ways this attitude is exhibited in our society?

- Why should the "most toys" attitude be considered foolishness by Christians?

Looking at the Law

You shall not steal.

What does this mean? We should fear and love God so that we do not take our neighbor's money or possessions, or get them in any dishonest way, but help him to improve and protect his possessions and income.

You shall not covet ...

What does this mean? We should fear and love God so that we do not scheme to get our neighbor's possessions, or get it in a way which only appears right, but help and be of service to him in keeping them.

Matthew 16:24-26

• What point is Jesus making about priorities?

• What non-material things might we need to "deny" in order to follow Jesus?

• When does desire for anything turn into sin?

- When can the desire for personal achievement turn into sin?

Looking at Life

Video 6B

- What were some examples of coveting?

- What is good or bad about the way Catherine works toward the goal of a better center?

- Patrice wants a raise. What is right or wrong with this desire?

- Julia wants to improve her appearance. What is right or wrong with this desire?

- How did Tommy give glory to God when Kendall asked him to "charge for some of the free stuff?"

- If you could share words of wisdom with any of these individuals, what would you say?

Video 6C

- What were some examples of desires becoming sinful?

- What were some examples of stealing?

- What type of thinking leads us to falsely believe "the ends justify the means?"

- How did each of the person's actions exhibit a lack of trust in God?

📖 Matthew 6:25-27, 33-34
📖 Matthew 7:7-12
- What is Jesus teaching us about our desires?

- How could each individual have pursued his or her desire within God's will?

- How can we respond in faith when God tells us "no"?

Video 6D

- What should Catherine do now?

- What should Patrice do now?

- What strength does God's grace bring when we have sinned?

Living Grace-fully with Our Desires

- How does living under the cross of forgiveness make a difference in your continuing struggle to live grace-fully and according to the will of God?

Turn back to the list of things you would like to achieve in the next 10 years on page 73. Think about anything you would like to add or delete from the list. Then take a moment to pray. Ask for the Holy Spirit to help you give glory to God and live in a God-pleasing manner.

Video 6E

How would you respond in the spirit of the commandment to each of the following situations?

- **Julia and Al discuss swimming camp.**

- **Baines has ball tickets.**

> What would you do if you were Baines?

> What would you do if your were Tommy?

> What would you do if you were Kendall?

Living Grace-fully in the Coming Days

Rockefeller was one asked, "How much money do you need to be happy?" He said, "Just a little bit more." Eighty-seven percent of all college graduates interviewed on why they chose the career they did said it was because of the money they hoped to earn!

- **What was the motivating reason for the career choice you made?**

- **What would you tell someone who asked you, "What should be the main motivating force behind why I choose to do what I do?" Do you think your answer coincides with the commandments we've just studied?**

- **On a continuum from 1 to 10, regarding the subject of trusting that God will provide for your needs, how would you rank yourself (10 being the most trusting)?**

Today, tomorrow, throughout this week, whenever you doubt God's promise to care for you, whisper, "Get thee hence, Satan, in the Name of Jesus Christ."

Video 6F

Living grace-fully is a process that will take the rest of our lives. Repentance and forgiveness should always be followed by a promise (to one's self if no one else) to do better. Of course, the good intention does not guarantee success. Success in keeping the will of God comes only through the power of the Spirit.

Paul said, "We died to sin; how can we live in it any longer? Or don't you know that all of us who were baptized into Christ Jesus were baptized into His death? We were therefore buried with Him through baptism into death in order that, just as Christ was raised from the dead through the glory of the Father, we too may live a new life" (Romans 6:2- 4). We are assured that our resurrection to new life begins now. It is in living out our "deadness" to sin and our new life in Christ that we live grace-fully.